AF480918

Hey, hi!

Thank you for trusting us with your story time. We certainly hope you enjoy the story ahead! A few quick reminders before you begin-

 Be sure to flip to the back for some fun facts (some might say the funnest), to learn more about our bud Mungo and to meet the author and illustrator!

 **Hey, Hi!** Books are books that give. A portion of proceeds from every book sold goes toward helping others! Proceeds from this book will go toward the education of children in need. We greatly appreciate your support.

 Be sure to visit our website at **heyhimediallc.com** for more!

Dedication:
-To all past, present and future patriots!-

Published by Hey, Hi Media LLC - A Family and Children's Media Company
All rights reserved. Copyright 2023.

Heyhimediallc.com

INDEPENDENCE? CONSIDER IT DECLARED!

Written by Scott Watkins

Illustrated by Casey Pipetti

Hey, Hi!

A Family Media Company

Come all you children and lend me your ears,
I shall tell you a tale that will bring you to tears!

No, not of sadness but of gladness and elation.
For this is the tale of a great deliberation.

The year is 1776, the place? Philadelphia.

After years of unrest, the colonies have had it
up to here - I tell ya!

The representatives gathered from each of the original 13.

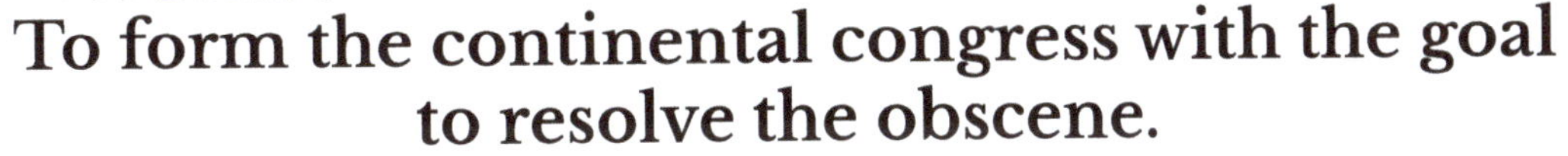

To form the continental congress with the goal
to resolve the obscene.

They've been taxed and attacked and aren't even considered true countrymen.
They have no representation in parliament and no means to an end.

King George is a tyrant -
some wholeheartedly agree.

Yet some do not think so to a certain degree.

You see, most colonists have been raised to show loyalty
to the crown.

But recent events are turning loyalties upside down.

A new nation should be born! Some passionate folks
do exclaim.

But others say that means death, with treason to blame!

So first, they shall try a diplomatic approach.

They send an olive branch that's met only
with reproach.

A great debate takes place as our congress
continues to stew.

What's next? What's best?
What should we do?

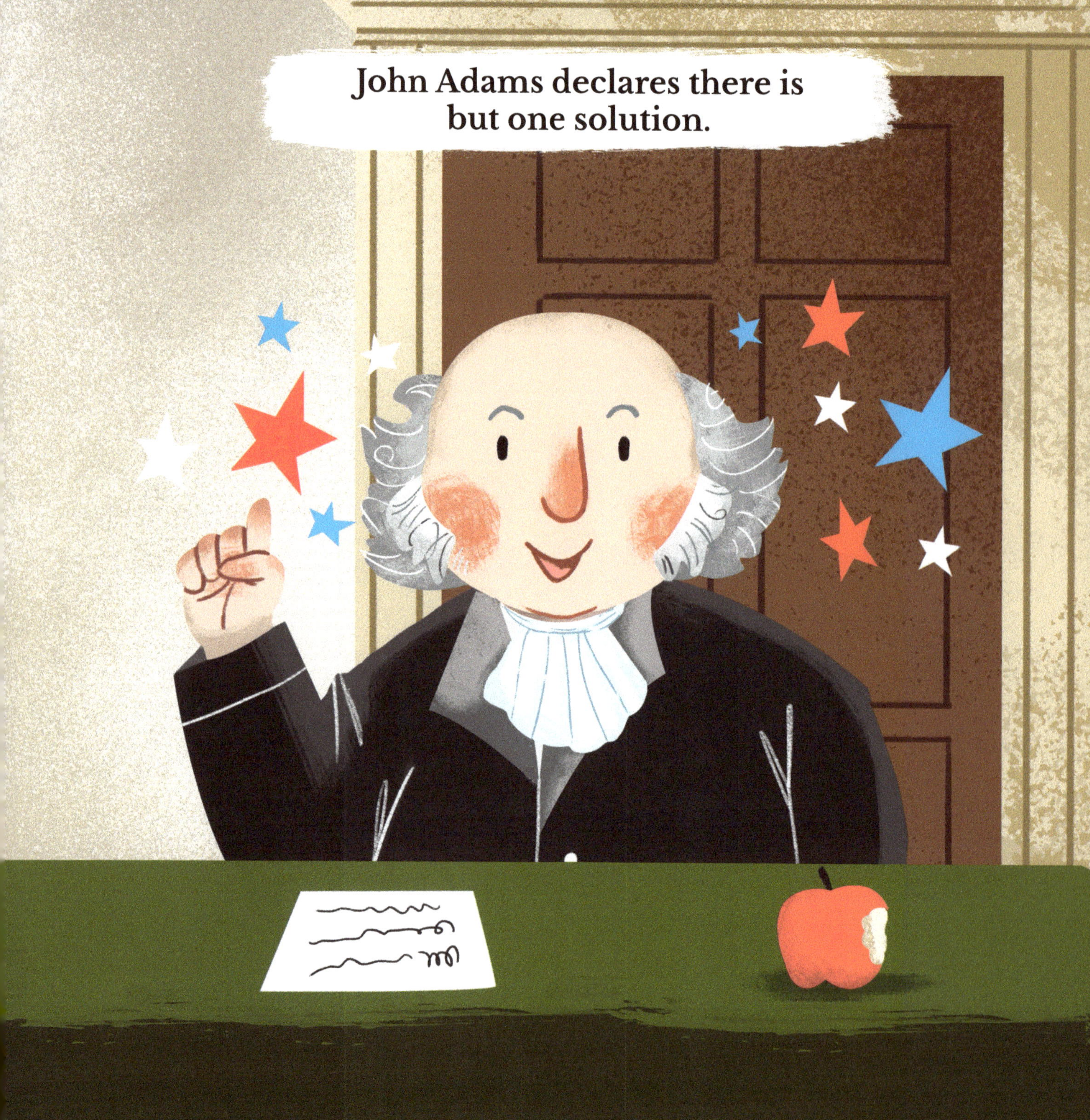

John Adams declares there is
but one solution.

We shall declare our independency, free from parliamentary institution.
One nation we shall be, a place to call our true homeland.

It will come at a cost but now is time to take a stand.

They knew such a declaration would be
met with war and despair.

But they're left without options and the thought of true
freedom rings in the air.

Thomas Jefferson is selected as the official pen.

He speaks of life, liberty, and the pursuit of happiness for all men!

CONSIDER
INDEPENDENCE...
DECLARED!

A heavy debate ensues but liberty ultimately succeeds. The declaration of independence is final but we're by no means out of the weeds.

War is ahead and everyone knows it.

But there's no going back. No thought of forfeit.

On July 2nd it's voted, and on the
4th formally announced.

The colonies were independent,
Britain officially renounced!

What happens next is a story for
another time.

Until then, I leave you with
just one last rhyme.

I mentioned before, this story should bring
you all elation!

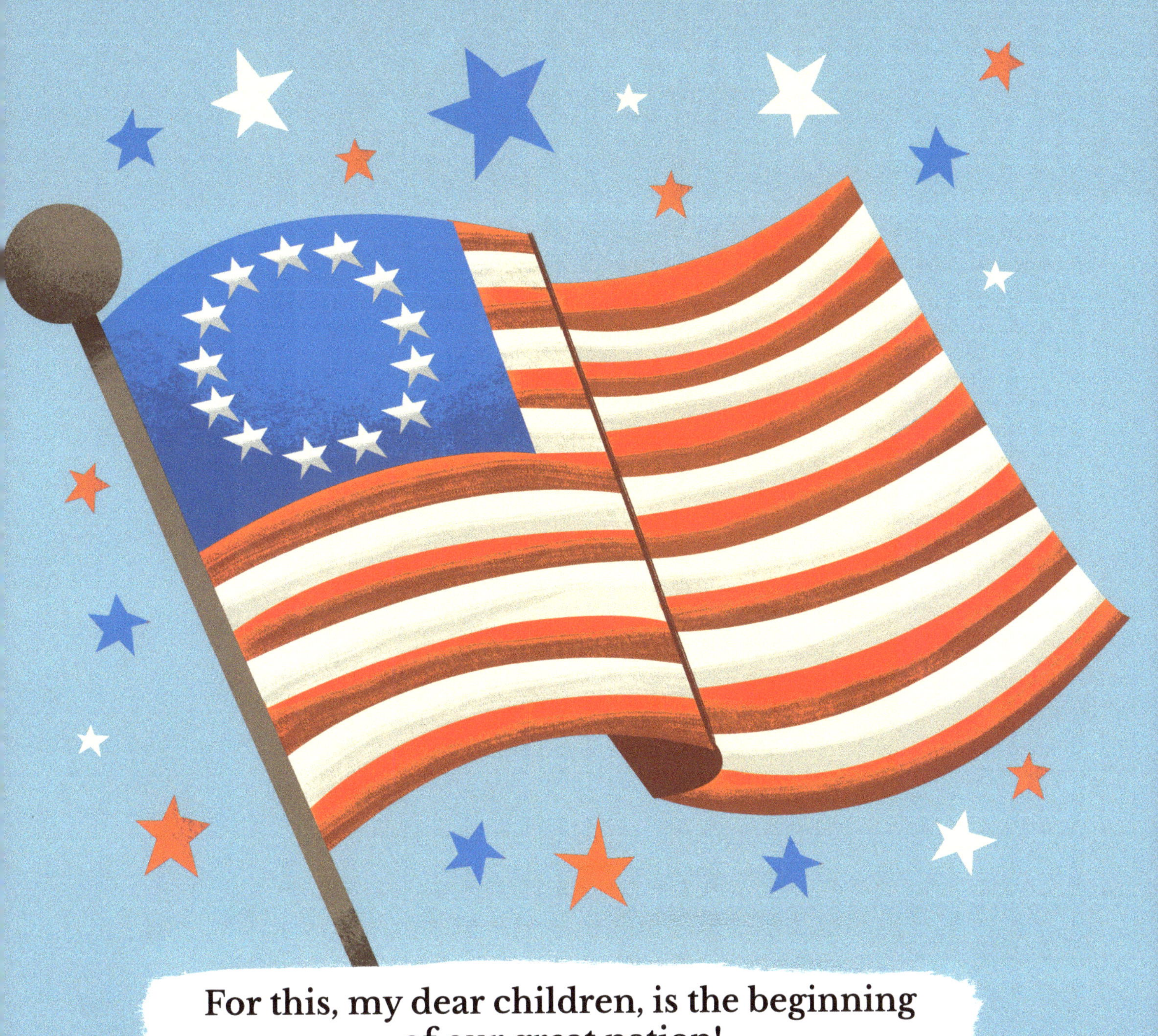

For this, my dear children, is the beginning
of our great nation!

The Funnest of Facts!

① Teamwork Makes the Dream Work!

The Continental Congress appointed "The Committee of Five" with the goal of creating a document that told Great Britain and the World, why the colonies should be independent. The Committee of Five consisted of John Adams, Roger Sherman, Benjamin Franklin, Robert Livingston and Thomas Jefferson. The committee appointed Thomas Jefferson to write the document. Afterward, Jefferson asked Benjamin Franklin and John Adams to review and make changes.

② Enough Said.

The Declaration of Independence only has 1,320 words! That's just a few more words than this book!

③ Happy 2nd of July?

In a letter written to his wife, John Adams predicted that future generations of Americans would celebrate Independence Day, just like we do today! However, he got the date wrong. He thought July 2nd would be the official "Independence Day" celebrated, but it ended up being July 4th .

④ Declared Now, Signed Later

Speaking of July 4th - did you know that is not the actual day the Declaration of Independence was signed? The Declaration was officially adopted July 4th. The adoption of the final wording meant independence from Great Britain was officially announced. However, it was not actually signed until August 2, 1776.

Meet Mungo!

Did you notice our tiny revolutionary, Mungo?

Mungo will be joining us for all our history adventures!

Guess what?

Mungo was an actual squirrel from revolutionary times! Squirrels were very popular pets in those days. One of the biggest squirrel fans was Benjamin Franklin! He actually gifted Mungo to a young girl while he was living in England as a diplomat.

About the Author & Illustrator

Scott Watkins

Don't let the beard, tattoos, general adult responsibilities or age fool you. Scott is a large child at heart. Scott's love for storytelling began at a young age and has grown into a mission to impact and enrich the lives of others through fun and meaningful stories.

Although Scott is not a #1 Bestselling New York Times Author, his wonderful wife and mother say he's a #1 best seller in their eyes. Scott calls a little town outside of Pittsburgh, PA home with his wife and darling daughter. When not writing, Scott loves preaching, learning, sports and anything outdoors (or as they'd say in the old days "out of doors").

 @ heyhimedia    heyhimediallc.com

Casey Pipetti

Casey has been drawing since she could hold a pencil - and she never stopped. Most days you can find her diligently toiling away over her Wacom tablet in her home office. She is inspired by cute and colorful things, animals, vintage illustrations, and contemporary art.

Despite her colorful and whimsical style, she really enjoys spooky things and rainy days. Born in Hollidaysburg, PA and a resident of Pittsburgh for a half-decade, she is happy to call Pennsylvania her home. When she isn't working (which is rare) she is gaming, playing guitar, walking her golden retriever, or fueling her curiosity about life by reading and studying various topics.

 @ happygoatdraws    happygoatdraws.com